POCKET IMAGES

# Colyton & Seaton

This interesting water-colour, c. 1830, although primitive, is the only known picture of the Mansion House, the property with the wall on the right-hand side. Notice the back slope of the shingle bar; the Mansion House stood on a holding named Clarke's Tenement, which was a section of this back slope. The house was named because of its association with the Willoughby family and the lords of the manor, the Trevelyans. It was used as a summer residence by the ladies of the families. The Trevelyans owned the whole beach, so privacy could be maintained, and it remained the only house apart from the Preventive Men's House (for the revenue men), seen at the end of the shingle bar. The section of marsh with grazing cattle next to the river was named Sheeps Marsh, and the section with the hayrick was Sea Marsh. The mansion house was converted into the Assembly Rooms in the middle of the nineteenth century, and the Beach Hotel was added to it on the seaward side. Today the back slope from Trevelyan Road to Beach Road is covered with houses, and its story over the past 140 years is one of many opportunities lost to the town.

POCKET IMAGES

# Colyton & Seaton

Ted Gosling

NONSUCH

*Dedicated to Derek Good and John and Wendy Underwood who have contributed much to their native village of Beer.*

First published 1994
This new pocket edition 2007
Images unchanged from first edition

Nonsuch Publishing
Cirencester Road, Chalford
Stroud, Gloucestershire, GL6 8PE
www.nonsuch-publishing.com

Nonsuch Publishing is an imprint of NPI Media Group

© Ted Gosling, 1994

The right of Ted Gosling to be identified as the Author
of this work has been asserted in accordance with the
Copyrights, Designs and Patents Act 1988.

British Library Cataloguing in Publication Data.
A catalogue record for this book is available from the British Library.

ISBN 978-1-84588-411-6

Typesetting and origination by NPI Media Group
Printed in Great Britain

# Contents

The girls pictured here are competitors in a 'Sweetheart of the Forces' competition, held at a British Legion fête in Seaton cricket field, c. 1946. They are, from left to right: Mary Taylor, Mary Otton, Vera Larcombe and Daphne Real.

Seaton football, 27 May 1943. At the back, from left to right are: Ken Tolman, John Collins, Cyril Legg, Mr Charles, Harry Leyman, Mr Northcott, Ernest Brown, Mr Legg. Centre: Fred Sellers, Arthur Restorick, Wallace Anning, Bill Pugh, Eddie Parker. Front: Harold Rodgers, Nobby Clarke, Toby White, -?-, Bert Cullen, -?-, Herman Anning, Maurice Bevan. Stan Parker and Dave Newberry are standing with their backs to the camera.

# Introduction

Every book, as well as every human being, ought to be able to show some justification for existing. The value of a book is to be found in the worth of its content: in the enlightenment, diversion or consolation that it may be able to impart.

Just before I started on this preface, I was reading a fascinating little book written by Lady Bell in 1907, with one of those lovely titles typical of Victorian and Edwardian times, called Topics for Conversation. Her first topic is 'At the telephone; a warning'. She says: 'Those of us who are aged remember the time when there were no telephones. We liked that state of things better, most of us; and we say, at intervals, in a tone of dignified protest, that we do not like telephones, and that we really cannot stand motors.' While accepting that progress is inevitable, she goes on for twelve pages to explain her dislikes.

Another of her topics was the discussion of health, and she comments that she would like someone to protest against the extent to which the talk of health, or diet and the internal processes has infiltrated general conversation.

I mention these topics to show just a couple of the changes which have taken place in little more than a lifetime. In every aspect of life changes have been enormous, particularly in scientific and technological development. The importance of a book like this lies in the fact that it records pictorially many of the changes that have taken place.

Sir John Herschel coined the word 'photography' in 1839 and yet, when I look at volumes covering the First World War, I find them full of quite incredibly good photographs.

Ted Gosling is one of those people who had the foresight, and the collector's instinct, to save all the photographs and documents which came his way. Born locally, he has lived and worked in this area all his life. His jobs have involved a great deal of local travel and I suspect that he probably knows the whole district better than the back of his hand.

We are all fascinated, to some extent, by the past, particularly when that may include the lives of our parents and grandparents. When you look at the photographs, just see how many changes have taken place in the buildings, clothing, shoes, transport and shop fronts. You will find the experience rewarding, with not a few surprises.

Norman Whinfrey
Axmouth, 1994

R.H. and J. Folletts, Fore Street, Seaton, c. 1898. Folletts were wine, spirit and beer merchants as well as being first class grocers and ironmongers. They also dealt in china and glass, and were seed and corn merchants. The low building next to Folletts was then occupied by T. Sloman, who had posting and livery stables. He also ran the town omnibus, with a fare of 3d to all parts of Seaton from the railway station. This building was demolished in 1902 and Seaton Town Hall was built on the site.

# One

# Colyton

Looking up from Market Place, Colyton, c. 1902. The property on the right was occupied then by the Devon constabulary. In the early years of the century, it was possible to stand in the middle of the road and gaze at the photographer. Trying this today would be suicidal.

This picture, taken from Queen Square, Colyton, in 1903, shows the Lion Inn, which was burnt down on 8 November 1908 and never rebuilt. Colyton Cottage is on the left in the foreground, and the Lion stood on the opposite side of Sidmouth Road. The Congregational chapel in the background was built in 1814 and enlarged in 1831. The shop on the right was then occupied by Frederick James Abrahams, who was a tailor.

Queens Square, Colyton, c. 1910.

*Above:* Looking down Sidmouth Road, Colyton, c. 1899. The workshop pictured on the right belonged to Mr Copp the blacksmith, and the building on the left was a lace factory.

*Below:* Market Place, Colyton, c. 1866. When this picture was taken, Colyton had a paper mill, a tannery, a brewery, a small foundry and three corn mills. Markets were held on Thursdays and Saturdays, and the streets were lit by gas.

*Above:* Looking down to the Colcombe Castle Hotel, Colyton, c. 1897.

*Left:* Bear Inn, King Street, Colyton, c. 1908. At the time of this picture the landlord was George Warry Bull.

*Opposite above:* R.H. and J. Follet of Colyton were family grocers and ironmongers.

*Opposite below:* This panoramic view of Colyton, taken from Kingdon Hill in around 1932, is of special interest because it shows Colyton station, closed in 1966 by the infamous Beeching Axe, to be full of goods waggons. This is an indication of the part the busy branch line played in the economic life of both Seaton and Colyton.

Colyton's two old fire engines which went out of use in around 1910. Note the handcart which carried the various accessories, and which was pushed to the fire.

Colcombe Castle Hotel, Colyton, c. 1960. The Colcombe Castle was then a fully licensed residential and family hotel recommended by the AA and the RAC. The stone building on the right, once part of the stables of the Great House, was occupied by Colcombe Garage, owned by Percy Trivett.

Colyton Social Club, c. 1905. The club, which looks down into Colyton's town centre, has played a large role in the town's social life this century and was the HQ of the 3rd VBG Regiment. The thatched building with its corner just visible on the left went in road widening schemes, but the Old Compass pub in the left background is still there, albeit now a private residence.

The Square and High Street, Colyton, c. 1939.

*Left*: The Colyton Industrial and Provident Society was established in Colyton in 1894. Pictured here in 1920 are the staff members outside their shop in Sidmouth Road. From left to right: Mr Donald Purse, Mr Jay (the manager), Irene Restorick, Roy French, Norman Bishop and Harold Purse. The shop site is now a part of Hoechst Caram Tech UK Ltd factory.

*Below*: East Street, Colyton, c. 1910, a less-photographed part of the town. Woran's sadlers shop on the left has long since been a private residence.

St Andrew's Square, Colyton, c. 1906. The gate on the right led to the Colyton Foundry. At the time of this picture, the factories in Colyton included four grist mills – one on the River Coly, another on the Umborne and two in the town. There was also a tanyard and steam sawmills, as well as this foundry in St Andrew's Square.

View of Colyton taken from the church tower, c. 1899. The field in the background is now the home of Colyton Football Club. The tall chimney to the right, which was at Hamlin Mills, has now gone.

High Street, Colyton, 1918. The Colcombe Castle Hotel takes its name from one of the former homes of the Courtenay earls of Devon situated on the outskirts of the town on the road to Shute. The castle was allowed to fall into disrepair after the attainder and execution of Henry Courtenay in 1539, on a trumped-up charge of treason against Henry VIII. It was the revenues of some of Henry Courtenay's lands, bought back from the Crown, that allowed the Feoffees to do many of their good works for the town, including, in 1545, the founding of a grammar school, 'for the goodly and virtuous education of children in Colyton for ever'.

Fore Street, Colyton, c. 1910. The house on the left, named Oroolong, was then a girls' school, but it had formerly been the residence of Captain Henry Wilson, the discoverer of the Pelew Islands. The house was named by him in remembrance of the island on which he and his crew landed when they escaped from their ship the Antelope, which was wrecked on 10 August 1783. The Captain and his crew were kindly received by the natives and on 26 August 1783 Abba Thulle, the king, presented the islands to Captain Wilson for England.

Taken above Chantry Bridge on the footpath that leads towards Southleigh, c. 1920. Note that the chimney at Hamlin Mills had gone.

East Street, Colyton, c. 1959. The Old Bakehouse was then called The Gay Dolphin. It was a highly successful café, with bed and breakfast accommodation and also sold fish and chips. The White House in the background was still a private residence.

19

*Above*: On 13 May 1924 it was decided by the Feoffees of Colyton that a public building for the benefit of the town should be erected on the site of the old Market House. This photograph, taken that year, shows the old building that was demolished to make way for the present town hall.

*Opposite below:* This sweet shop, which belonged to a Mr and Mrs Anning, stood on the site of the present Colyton Feoffees' Town Hall. They made their own sweets, including brown and white peppermints.

*Right:* Ruins of Colcombe Castle, Colyton, c. 1910. The castle was originally built by Hugh de Courtenay and at one time was in the possession of Sir William Pole, the historian. Although he restored it, it fell into decay after the Civil War.

*Below:* Interior view of the parish church of St Andrew, Colyton, c. 1904.

One of the oldest photographs of Colyton, c. 1859. This revealing picture of Market Place shows an era of thatched cottages, very different from the Colyton of today.

Colyton, c. 1948. Looking from Queens Square into Church Street, this picture is of special interest as it shows the old White Hart Inn, the thatched building on the left, which was badly burnt in the 1960s and is now a private residence.

## Two

# Seaton

Looking up Fore Street, Seaton, February 1966. Prospect House in The Square was then occupied by Boots, and the estate agents Allen and Taylor were trading from the premises in the left foreground. You can see that there was less traffic about then, and people could cross the road with ease. At the time of this picture, the Royal Clarence was 100 years old, and nobody had thought of changing the name of one of our oldest establishments to its present ugly title.

Montpellier School for Girls, Seaton, Devon, c. 1908. Built in 1824 as a private residence, this was one of the first houses in the town to be built of brick, so was known as Brick House. During the 1890s it became Friedenham Seaside School for Girls, changing its name to Montpellier School about 1900. Later it became Ferris and Prescott the drapers and after they ceased trading it was occupied by Barclays Bank and the Job Centre.

Classrooms at the rear of Montpellier School, Seaton, c. 1908. The principal of this girls' school was a Miss Mary Grover, who was assisted by five resident mistresses and visiting masters. Pupils were prepared for the junior and senior Cambridge and London Matriculation, and also for advanced examinations in music (London RAM). The school provided a thorough education for daughters of gentlemen.

Pupils' sitting room, Montpellier School for Girls, Seaton, c. 1908. The school was specially recommended for the children of Anglo-Indians and the motto was mens sana in corpore sano.

The old West Walk, Seaton, c. 1906. At the time of this photograph, there was a well-defined promenade stretching from Seaton Hole to the beach opposite the railway station. A large portion of this esplanade lay under the shelter of the West Cliff, and seats were provided at frequent intervals. Unfortunately, most of this walk was destroyed during a severe gale in 1915.

Seaton beach, c. 1885. At this date fishing was a major industry in the town, and the beach was a busy place, packed with fishing boats. The Bath House, seen here in the centre, provided both residents and visitors with hot and cold sea-water baths. It was run by a Mrs Woodgate, who charged 2s 6d for a hot bath, 2s for a tepid bath and 1s for a cold one. If you ordered a bath but did not take it, she charged you half price.

*Opposite above:* Looking along the East Walk to Haven Cliff, c. 1926. The Beach Hotel, pictured here, was the resort's premier hotel. Jimmy Donovan and his Broadcasting Band played weekly during the season for both residents and locals.

*Opposite below:* White Cliff and Seaton Hole c. 1885. You can see from this photograph how much erosion has taken place during the past hundred years.

Trevett's car park and garage, Harbour Road, January 1964. The model railway firm Peco were in the premises now occupied by Leisure and Pleasure, and the Rainbow complex now sprawls over what was Trevett's filling station.

Trevett's car park, Seaton, January 1964, looking toward White Cliff residential home. This car park is now the site of Fosseway Court.

Harbour Road, Seaton, 1962. At this time the road was correctly named Station Road, and the property on the right was called the Royal Clarence Hotel. Mettams Gift Shop occupied what is now the 4 Cs fish and chip shop.

Looking up Seafield Road, Seaton, c. 1962. The boundary wall of Seafield House can be seen on the left-hand side of Seafield Road. Seafield House was destroyed by a German bomber during the Second World War, and the site is now the Jubilee Gardens.

Aerial view of Seaton, c. 1957. During the post-war years, great social changes took place, and since this photograph new housing estates have spread out beyond the former boundaries of the town. Although at this date Everest Drive had been completed, the development of land around the cricket and football fields had not yet taken place. The Regal Cinema can be clearly seen in the centre, with the row of houses on Violet Terrace running beside it. Both the cinema and Violet Terrace were demolished in the early 1970s. The land now occupied by Fosseway Court was then Trevett's car park, and the building in the centre was a filling station.

*Opposite above:* Warner's Holiday Camp, Seaton, January 1964. It took three months to build the original Warner's Holiday Camp, which opened at Easter 1935, for 200 people. Billy Butlin was on the board of the company, which was led by Captain Harry Warner, and he paid a visit to Seaton to watch progress. The fifty men who helped to build this Warner's camp formed the nucleus of the team who in a few months were to build the first Butlin's camp at Skegness. The original Seaton camp was damaged by fire during the late 1930s, and during the Second World War was home to various forces, including Polish troops and the Americans.

*Opposite below:* Seaton Pastimes, 1961.

*Left:* Zions Hill, Seaton, c. 1895. Zions Hill was the path that led down from Seaton Hole to the beach.

*Below:* The Square, Seaton, c. 1910. Gosney the chemist occupied the shop on the left, now Byrne-Jones, and Lloyds Bank still occupies the same site today. The bank manager then was a Mr Ernest Wyatt.

Looking towards the Royal Clarence Hotel, 1873. The Royal Clarence was completed in 1866, and the manager at the time of this photograph was William Loud. The house on the left, now the site of Bric-a-Brac, was called Marine Cottage, and was occupied by a Miss E. Otton, who kept a lodging-house. Next to the Royal Clarence is Seaton House, which is now occupied by solicitors Milford and Dormer. At the time this photograph was taken it belonged to Henry Wylde, who died in 1876. Henry Wylde was a 'gentleman in ordinary' to Queen Victoria at the Chapel Royal, St James's Palace, and a music teacher. He must have retired to Seaton.

Looking up Fore Street, Seaton, c. 1885. The thatched buildings on the right were then occupied by T. Sloman's posting and livery stables. Sloman's also ran the town omnibus. These stables were demolished in 1902, to make way for the new town hall. The shop on the corner of Cross Street was then Gould's Cross Street Machine Bakery. Gould and Son were high class bakers and confectioners, and their up-to-date bakery was fitted with all the latest machinery for the manufacture of bread.

Fore Street, Seaton, c. 1869. At the time of this photograph the house in the left foreground, named Prospect House, was used as wine vaults by Mitchell, Turner & Co. It was also occupied by a Mrs Hayworth, a lodging-house keeper whose husband kept a draper's shop in Fore Street. Further up the street on the left, Mr S. Gage had a family grocer's shop and sold foreign and British wines. Other Fore Street traders at that time included James Skinner, a baker and confectioner, Mr Perry, furnishing ironmonger, and Edward Overmass, a joiner and builder.

Gould's First Class Temperance Hotel, c. 1900. At the turn of the century, C.C. Gould, one of the town's leading citizens, ran this hotel on the site now occupied by Woolworths. The hotel provided good accommodation for visitors and included a fine restaurant, which was a popular meeting place for the people of Seaton.

The advertisement for Gould's Restaurant in Seaton was in a local guide of 1898. Gould's was the venue for all local occasions, including weddings, and was noted for excellent food and service.

*Above:* Seaview Terrace, Seaton, c. 1890. Sea Field in the foreground was still undeveloped.

*Left:* Haddington House, Queen Street, Seaton, c. 1898. The shop was occupied by Overmass and Sons, who were general house furnishers as well as being upholsterers, paper-hangers, and also undertakers. Removals were also carried out to all parts of the country by road and rail, and Overmass were well known for good service. Until recently, Haddington House was occupied by the showroom and offices of the SWEB.

*Opposite above:* Ferris and Prescott, Seaton, 25 November 1932. Mr A.J. Ferris and Mr W.H. Prescott, who had a drapers and outfitters shop in Montpellier House, Queen Street, are seen here with staff members.

Cliff Castle, Seaton. Cliff Castle was built by Joseph Good (1795-1874) in about 1825, and was originally plain fronted. When he sold the house, the new owner commissioned him to erect a castellated front. This photograph, taken in May 1935 when the house was floodlit for the Silver Jubilee week of King George V, was entered in the Amateur Photographer Silver Jubilee competition by H. Simpson of Sidmouth Street, Seaton.

Seaton, Marine Place, c. 1899. The drinking fountain to the right of the foreground was given to the town by Mr W.H. Willans, to mark the Diamond Jubilee of Queen Victoria in 1897. On the left of the picture is the wall of the Bath House, which was demolished in 1905.

The East Walk, Seaton, c. 1906. The ruthless pace at which we live today is so different from the leisurely world of Edwardian Seaton.

*Above*: Elizabeth Road, Seaton, 1950. Building operations for Elizabeth Road began in 1950 with the cutting of the new road from Harepath Road to Scalwell Lane. Pictured here is the road before the houses were built.

*Below*: Church Lane with St Gregory's, Seaton's parish church, in the background.

Manor Road, Seaton, 1907. The iron railings were removed during the Second World War.

Manor Road, Seaton, c. 1903. At the time of this photograph the house seen here, on the corner of Manor Road, was a private nursing home.

*Above*: Headlands and Wessiters Cottage, Seaton, c. 1910.

*Right*: Old Beer Road, Seaton, c. 1899.

Seaton, "In the Pines".

41

Seaton, the East Walk, c. 1960. The sea wall had not yet been built and people could sit in their cars and view the sea. The tea hut on the beach in the background was occupied by Jimmy Green from Beer, who served splendid cream teas and cakes on beach trays, with real china cups. Mrs Moore and Mrs Reed, who served the tea, are still remembered with great affection.

## Three

# The Villages

Beer village, 1895. The village is an essential part of the English landscape, and the quaint, charming fishing village pictured here holds a special place in the heart of all Devonians. At the time of this photograph, Beer was mainly populated by fishermen, quarrymen and farm workers. Change came very slowly to them, and the old village ways still remained. The folk of Beer then, as now, were warm-hearted people and strangers were always made welcome. Much has changed since the date of this picture; newcomers now outnumber the true natives and in many cases have abused the hospitality shown to them. Despite all, Beer people, still remain the salt of the earth, their talk has not yet lost the rich Devon accent, and they still retain the qualities of their forefathers.

Fore Street, Beer, c. 1902. The brook on the left supplied the village with a stream of pure water that flowed rapidly towards the beach. The stream still runs through the village, even in the driest of summers. The thatched cottages on the right were pulled down, and are now the site of the car park.

Shepherds Cottage, Beer, c. 1890. In the background you can see the shop belonging to Mr A. Northcott.

General view of Beer, c. 1890. Beautifully seated in a deep, narrow glen, Beer was a fishing village formerly in the tithing of the civil parish of Seaton. In November 1894 it was formed into a separate parish under the Local Government Act of the same year. At the time of this picture, Lord Clinton was lord of the manor and the main landowner.

Jake Blackmore's cottage, Steel's Court, Beer, c. 1910. Jake Blackmore, a well-known Beer character, was a fisherman. Steel's Court, which is now known as Otton's Court, was named after a shop owned by Dicky Steel which stood on the corner.

Ellesmere House, Beer, c. 1909. Before he moved to The Grange in 1911, Dr Edward Tonge lived at Ellesmere House. In this photograph his daughter Ethel is standing in the doorway.

*Right:* The sweet shop near the Fountain Head, Branscombe, c. 1930.

*Below:* Old cottages near the fountain head, Branscombe, c. 1928. The use of local materials was a distinctive feature in the cottages of Branscombe. The combination of stone, cob and thatch resulted in a pleasing picture, although at the time of this picture most of the inhabitants knew nothing of modern drainage systems, and the cottages could be damp and unhealthy. In recent years, careful restoration has corrected many of these inherent faults, but it has also unfortunately put them in a price range beyond the pocket of many locals.

Shepherds Cottage, Beer, c. 1912. Here we see Dr Tonge's children, Kenneth and Leila, with Biddie in the pram, posing in front of the cottage, which has always been a favourite subject for photographers.

Beer beach, c. 1929, showing the pole of the Washbourne memorial light. This lamp was presented to the village by a Mr Washbourne. The pole was 50 ft high and, when lined up with the village church, was used as a navigational aid by local fishermen.

*Above:* Beer beach, c. 1924. Beer Cove which formed then, as now, a haven of rest for the fishing boats, is a most picturesque spot. Walled in by massive chalk cliffs, it is the haunt of seagulls.

*Below:* Beer beach, c. 1929. Because of its sheltered position, Beer boats are often able to go out fishing when it is almost impossible to put off from the open beaches at Seaton and Sidmouth. Between the far point of Beer Head and the beach are smugglers caves which can only be reached by boat.

Colyford, c. 1905. Although Colyford itself was not a Roman settlement, the now-busy A3052 that runs through it was once a branch road of the Icknield Way that linked Seaton and the quarries at Beer with the rest of Roman Britain. The village seen here is little changed, apart from recent development in the field on the left.

Colyford, c. 1906. The thatched building on the right has vanished, and is now the site of the filling station. The local wheelwright operated from the building on the left.

Mary Broom's farmhouse fire-place, Axmouth, c. 1960. Above the mantelpiece is a rack for the long spits, used over wood fires. The floor has its original paving of irregularly shaped pieces of flat stone.

Axmouth village, c. 1955.

Axmouth village, c. 1959.

Steppes Lane, Axmouth, c. 1963.

St Michael's church, Axmouth, c. 1953. The thatched cottages you see on the right were unfortunately demolished and replaced with a more modern building.

Stafford House, Colyford, c. 1908. Once the home of J. Impey Scarbrough JP, Stafford House at the date of this photograph was occupied by local farmer Samuel Anning Seller.

The Golden Hind at Musbury was once known as the New Inn, and the landlady for many of the pre-war years was the popular Mrs Chard. Pictured here outside the pub in 1930 are, from left to right, Jack Hannar, Eileen Salter (née Rockett) and her father, Ernest Rockett.

*Four*

# The People

Beer Flower Show, August 1931. This photograph of Beer schoolgirls country dancing the 'Butterfly' is charming. There is no feeling at all that this picture was pre-arranged because it has life. It is a snatch of social history that gives the viewer a strong feeling of being there.

One of the earliest records of the Dare family shows that Captain William Dare emigrated from East Devon in 1680 and set up one of America's earliest inns, the Blue Anchor, in Pennsylvania. He moved to New Jersey and became a successful farmer and major employer. His descendants now number well over 1,000. In 1923, the Revd Alphonso Dare set up the Dare Family Association. A branch living near the Mississippi River meets annually in Indiana. In East Devon, information on the Dare family goes back to 1598, when it was recorded that a William Dare left his daughter Hannah a house, garden and orchard called Abbotts Place, in Seaton. His grandson, Nicholas Dare, was another notable member of the family. A trader, he travelled throughout the West Country, delivering nets to Dartmouth and Kingsbridge in particular. He was so respected that during the Civil War he was granted a special Royalist pass. This was found in the roof of a cottage pulled down in 1839, possibly Abbotts Place. The museum at Seaton contains many articles owned by the Dare family, in particular a rum glass and a seal owned by Henry Watson Dare, born in 1782, a great seaman who traded out of Axmouth harbour.

He went to sea at the age of twelve, was shipwrecked off Brazil in 1812, wounded and captured by American pirates on his way home from El Salvador, returning to England eventually after an exchange of prisoners. In 1813 he was at sea again carrying supplies to the army in Spain, and in 1815, off Cuba, was again attacked by pirates who plundered his ship. He and his sons George and Henry continued to sail ships to many parts until 1848 when he suffered 'extreme nervousness' and assigned his two ships, Harry and Flirt, to the management of James T. Trimmer, of London. One son, Henry, went to Australia, but returned to Seaton and is buried in the family grave. George went to the East Indies and China. Capt. Henry Watson Dare died in 1862 and is also buried at Seaton. His life was fairly well chronicled, but there is some mystery about his brother Batt, pictured here, who lived at Seaton and was undoubtedly a well-known and respected figure of the community.

Joseph Good, born in Seaton in 1795, was a prominent builder, architect and, at one time, banker. Highly respected and loved for his kindness and quiet helpfulness, he built Check House for Sir Walter Trevelyan and Seaforth Lodge for Lady Ashburton. The Castle, Cliff House - now Washington House and originally two two-storey houses - and Halcyon and Cliff Cottages were also designed by him. He lived at the Castle and his children were born there. It was only in later life, when he had to sell it, that he was commissioned by the new owner to build on the present ornate, castellated front. Joseph owned much of the land around Cliff House, and he gave a strip of it to the town for a roadway - Castle Hill - as a link between the front and Beer Road. He died in 1875, about six years after this photo was taken by his son, Samuel Good, Seaton's first photographer. Samuel had set up in Axminster as a watchmaker and jeweller, but he was keen on photography and when he moved to Fore Street, Seaton, he made this interest part of his business. Apart from recording events and scenes of local interest he took many portraits, and used a cheap method which enabled ordinary people to have their pictures taken.

W. and F. Copp, pictured here in 1905, were blacksmiths in Sidmouth Road, Colyton. Here, amid the flying sparks and hot metal, they played an important part in the economy of Colyton in the days when the role of the horse was supreme.

The Seaton Scout Band on parade in 1913, with scout-master Revd Mr Robinson. The goat must have been their mascot.

*Left:* Reginald Wilkie Gosney. The son of a Seaton chemist, Reginald Gosney became a Second Lieutenant. in the First World War. He was on the Indian Army Reserve of officers, attached to the 76th Punjabis, and in 1915 was transferred to Mesopotamia where he took part in the capture of Kut and the ill-advised advance to Baghdad. After the capture of Kut, the British Forces, with a rifle strength of 13,000, advanced to attack the Turkish position at Ctesiphon. The Turks numbered more than 18,000 and after the battle on 22 November 1915 the British retreated with a loss of more than 4,500 men. Casualties and the dead were either left or buried by the Turks, with no regard to identification. Lt. Gosney, who was mentioned in despatches, was killed in the battle of 22 November, and his name is inscribed on the Basra memorial in Iraq to those who have no known grave.

*Below:* Miss Ada Skinner, pictured here in 1920, was the daughter of James William Skinner, who ran a baker's shop at Salcombe House, Seaton. James, who died in 1913 aged eighty-seven, also had four sons. Ada Louise never married; she kept a dairy at Salcombe House, and died in 1945, also aged eighty-seven years.

Colyton Rifle Team, 1903, with their trophies won at Battalion and Devon County meetings. Back row, from left to right: Pte. S. Milton, Sgt. G. White, Sgt. Lockyer, Pte. W. Richards, Pte. G.W. Dare, Pte. A.J. White, Pte. F. White. Middle row: Sgt-Inst. Lilley, Capt. Cosens, Col-Sgt. Spurway. Front row: Pte. S. Hooper, L. Cpl. E.E. Richards, Pte. E. Snell.

This postcard, which was printed in 1907, celebrated the extraordinary fact that during the previous hundred years there had been only three vicars of Colyton.

1067 ATC Squadron was formed at Colyton Grammar School during the Second World War, but did not draw exclusively on school pupils for its members. The three officers in the front row, all members of the school staff, are Mr Jowett, Mr Montgomery and Mr Slade.

This picture, thought to be of Sports Day winners at Colyton Grammar School in about 1930, shows some of the winners' shields at the front. Made by Mr W.H. Creswick, handicraft teacher at the school between 1928 and 1949, like all his work they attracted considerable attention and praise. Among those pictured are staff members Bill Jowett and Miss Passmore, centre and seated, and Becky Parker, Ena Richards, Olive Brown, Doris Hayman, Winnie Sweetland, Hilda Long, George Loud, Bagwell, Hartley and Tucker.

Ship Inn 'B' Darts Team, 1952. The team is outside the Ship Inn. Back row, from left to right: Ted Board, Eric Childs (landlord), John Purse. Front row: Dave Vaughan, Herbie Clement, Ray Gush, Freda Childs (landlady), Bill Busby.

Feoffees' swimming pool, Colyton, c. 1930. The pool was opened on 8 August 1914, and was for the benefit of Colyton Grammar School and the inhabitants of Colyton. This pool, beside the Shute stream near Horse Lane Road, came under the management of the Feoffees. It was 60 ft long and 25 ft wide; it had concrete sides and for flushing purposes was connected to a drain that ran 500 yd across a field. It drew its water from the Umborne Brook, which was much cleaner than the nearby Coly.

*Above*: Seaton Urban District Councillors gathered together for the last time on 5 April 1974. The Seaton Urban District Council was formed in 1894 under the provisions of the Local Government Act, 1894. This superseded the old Local Board, constituted in 1878. Following local government reorganization the urban council ceased to exist. Its power went to the East Devon District Council, and the new Seaton Town Council lost control of all the resort amenities. Pictured here, from left to right: Mr W. Woolland, Mr G. Wilder, Mrs E. Apthorp (vice-chairman), Mr G. Lever (financial officer), Mr Harry Garrod (clerk), Mr Cyril Maud (deputy clerk), Mr George Clare (chairman), Mr Maxwell Smith, Mr A. Stenner, Mr T.W. Holland, Mrs Mavis Williamson, Mr D. Isgrove, Mr J.F. Allison (surveyor).

*Below*: My many friends will know that the Costa Brava, that beautiful Catalan sea coast of Spain, is my favourite holiday destination. Pictured here in the 1960s are Seaton boys Sandy Dack, on the left, and Ross Dack, enjoying a night out in one of Lloret's many bodegas, and also the charm of the local senoritas.

Bovey Pond, Beer, 1 March 1929. Severe weather during the early months of 1929 froze Bovey Pond enough for ice-skating. Here we see Dr Edward Tonge, the local doctor, making full use of the unusual conditions.

Bovey Pond, Beer, 4 March 1929. Many local people skated on Bovey Pond during the intense frost of that time. When it grew dark the ice was lit with Chinese lanterns and people skating with torches. During the day parties were held, and this group looking pleasant, cosy and sociable were members and friends of Dr Tonge's family.

Beer Cubs setting off to camp, 25 August 1929. The camp was held at Weston Gap.

Beer Cubs at Weston Camp, August 1929.

With the outbreak of the Second World War, Sydney Pritchard and his brother William won a contract to produce shell fuses and aircraft components. Their factory in Holloway, North London, was moved to the garage in The Square, Branscombe. Pictured here are some of the workers they employed, playing an important part in the war effort.

The Seaton Royal Observer Corps, c. 1943. The observers pictured here at their post on Clay Common rendered valuable service during the Second World War. There were observer posts over the entire country, where a day and night watch was kept for the sight or sound of enemy aircraft. Britain's defences were set in motion by these lonely and devoted watchers in their far-flung outposts, as they plotted the course of any enemy raiders.

Nestles munitions factory, Branscombe, c. 1943. Morale in the factory was high, with everyone united in a common cause and working hard. Loudspeakers played 'Music While You Work', which at times drowned the din of the machines.

During the First World War, Ryalls Court, Seaton, became a military hospital. Most of the patients were fairly straightforward cases, but there were some with multiple gunshot wounds. The boys were only too glad to escape from France for a time, from the horrors of trench warfare. Pictured here, with Dr Tonge sitting in the middle of the front row, are nurses, staff and patients in 1917.

Axmouth Home Guard, c. 1942. The Home Guard played an important part in the village war effort, and holds an honoured place in local history. Formed in 1940, they were first known as the LDV (Local Defence Volunteers). Pictured here are: Back row, from left to right: Jeff Puddicombe, Gordon Hunt, Ray Hunt, Lesley Hunt, Mr Mann senior, Mr Mann junior. Middle row: Herbie Clement, Jack Good, Ted Snell, Jim Cross, Jim Board, Ken Morgan, Mr Mann. Front row: Frank Snell, Harry Newbery, Len Weekes, the Revd Mr Swift, Howie (Harry) Owen, Ken Webber, Victor Worden.

Colyton Home Guard, c. 1943. The plan of raising Local Defence Volunteers in 1940 met with an immediate response from all over the country. Their name was soon changed to the Home Guard, although they were affectionately known as 'Dads' Army'. By the end of that year, the Home Guard numbered one and a half million men, and during the preparations for D-Day in 1944 they took over most of the security duties in the country. These men from Colyton played an important part in the Second World War, and after their final muster in 1945 much appreciation was felt by all for the voluntary work they had done during the difficult days of war.

*Above:* The children of Axmouth celebrating the coronation of Edward VII. The king was crowned in 1902, and the children of Axmouth village were assembled at the school to have this photograph taken by George Barton, the Seaton photographer. He left behind a picture of great charm, depicting a quaint old-fashioned group, the girls in their ankle-length frocks and white pinafores, and the boys in hobnailed boots. It must have been a memorable day for the children, whose lives were restricted by poverty and other hardships. Occasions like this were an escape from the narrow world in which they lived.

*Opposite above:* Charles Chapple, Beer fisherman, c. 1948. Born in Beer on 4 January 1876, Charles was the fourth son of James Chapple, a fisherman of Beer. Charles Chapple, like all Beer boys, was born for the sea and started fishing at the age of twelve as 'The Boy' in a local trawler. When he was nineteen he joined the Royal Navy and trained as a stoker. He was rated Stoker Petty Officer on 7 April 1906 and retired from the Royal Navy with the rank of Stoker Chief Petty Officer in 1919. While in the RN he was landed in the Naval Brigade and was a fireman on one of the railway steam engines that hauled the heavy naval guns to 'Spion Kop', which earned him a special commendation. Later he saw action in the battle of Jutland and more war service in the new Torpedo boats; finally he qualified in the use of oil-fired boilers. On his retirement to Beer he operated and owned an 18 ft motor boat, the Kathleen, taking fishing trips in the bay. He was a well-known and colourful personality, who died in the late 1950s.

*Opposite below:* Seaton Beach, c. 1910. The house in the centre background was then named Cliff House. It was a small hotel owned by Mr H.A. Good.

*Above:* Beer WI folk dancing team, 4 June 1930.

*Left:* Jim and Alice Gosling, 1929. Jim and Alice were the first people to live in Eyewell Green, Seaton. In this photograph, taken in local photographer George Barton's studio, they are proudly posing with their first son, Ted. Jim, who came from a Colyton family, married Alice in 1928. He died in 1992 having enjoyed sixty-four years of marriage.

Axmouth Gospel Hall and St Michael's church, Axmouth, c. 1947. These are the combined Sunday schools, together with children of Seaton, at Seaton Congregational church for tea party and lantern slide show. Axmouth children, second table back from front, on the far side, from left to right: Nancy Sweetland, Ann Real, Ivy Beasley, -?-, June Clement. Near side: Lavinia Blackmore, Maureen Humphrey, Pat Dack, Ruth Newbery, Faith Griffith, Rosemary Spiller, Mary Millman, Barbara Spiller, Celia Morgan. Near full table, far side: Bruce Dack, Robin Legg, Albert Snell, Leslie Legg, Mervyn Legg, Ross Dack, Michael Sweetland, Herbie Sweetland. Near side: Ted Humphrey, Paul Northcott, Raymond Puddicombe, John Webber, Brian Tipper, Roger Webber.

*Above:* Beer Cubs camping at Weston Gap, August 1927. The Cubs are, from left to right: Philip Miller, Derick Good and Frank Sydenham.

*Left:* Dr Tonge, the Beer doctor is pictured here with some of the Beer Scouts in 1914. the boy to Dr Tonge's right is holding a small statue, so this could have been an award presentation ceremony.

*Above:* Seaton Scouts, Vicarage Field, Seaton, c. 1914. In August 1907, twenty boys, led by two men, pitched their tents on Brownsea Island in Dorset. The boys were gathered from all walks of life, and for two weeks they learnt to live in the open and to cultivate comradeship. From this small beginning the Boy Scout movement was born, and Baden Powell, their leader, was on his way to becoming a world figure. The first Seaton Boy Scout troop was formed during April 1913, and here we have some of the first Scouts, with chaplain Revd R.S. Robinson.

*Right:* Nurse Richards, Seaton, c. 1938. Nurse Richards, who came from Wales to become Seaton's District Nurse, gave many years of service to the community. She is pictured with her bicycle and basket, as so many will remember her, with that cheerful grin and no-nonsense look.

Sir Walter Trevelyan's School, Seaton, c. 1910.

Pupils at Beer School, c. 1935. Note the young Roy Chapple, first left in the second row.

Seaton boys c. 1947, from left to right: D. Chown, D. Jones, Ted Gosling, Lyle Jones.

Seaton, West Walk, c. 1946, from left to right: Richard Way, Ted Gosling, Fred Cockram and Len Pritchard.

Mitchell Brothers, builders, c. 1937. Mitchell Brothers were responsible for building many of the houses in Seaton between the wars. They had offices in Harbour Road in a building now occupied by Leisure and Pleasure. The two workers on the ladders were Fred Quick and Ernest Rockett, who were painting the firm's offices.

Building Musbury Village Hall, c. 1928.

*Above:* Jack Widger and family, Seaton beach, c. 1959. Jack Widger from Axmouth had the beach hut and deckchair concession from the SUDC. He was a much-loved man and was well known to thousands of holiday-makers. He is pictured here as so many will remember him. From left to right: Una Board, May Widger, Jack Widger in beach hut, Ernest Widger, John Widger, Betty Widger (Jack's wife), Geoffrey Richards and June Richards.

*Right:* Henry Pavey, Seaton, c. 1969. Henry Pavey, who died aged 85 in 1976, was a local character. He served in the cavalry during the First World War, and saw action in France. In later years he kept pigs on a smallholding in Homer Lane, and carried containers full of pig swill on a cart, which was pulled by an old race horse with only one eye. One of the most enjoyable sights of the 1940s was Henry, sitting in his cart, charging up through the town—going so fast, in fact, that on one occasion the local police sergeant reported him for speeding.

Dr Tonge and his family, Beer beach, c. 1914. This picture, taken before the First World War, of Dr Tonge enjoying a picnic tea on Beer beach, captures the atmosphere of those golden Edwardian days.

Dr Edward Tonge with his family. A native of Yorkshire, Dr Tonge came to the Beer practice in 1897 and remained as the village doctor until his death in 1937. His name became synonymous with Beer, and when he died, aged sixty-four, the entire community mourned him.

The Turner family of Seaton, c. 1930. Taken in Stock Lane, this photograph shows several generations of the well-known building family. Arthur Turner is shown at the centre back, and his father and mother are sitting in the centre. Among the others are Benjamin Oakley Turner, Benjamin Turner the greengrocer, Sarah Anne, Agatha, Harry, Arthur, Vashti and Millicent, also Arthur Pearce and Hettie Pearce.

The Rockett family and friends outside the Hare and Hounds, Whitford, c. 1930. The group who have gathered for this picture include Bill Burrows, Ern Rockett and Tim Rockett.

*Left*: Herbert ('Bonny') Good, 1883–1962. A member of the regatta committee and the old rugby committee, Bonny will be remembered as much for his sense of humour as for his generous stature.

*Below*: Members of Beer WI pose for this photograph in 1932.

*Above:* Harry Lyons, c. 1942. Lyons was born in Long Lane, London, within the sound of Bow Bells. He joined the Royal Marines in August 1897, and saw action in all parts of the world. During the Boer War he was in the relief of Ladysmith. His time in the Marines covered twenty-two years. Harry Lyons joined the coastguards in May 1919, and during his first term of duty, which was in Ireland, many of the coastguards' homes were burnt down. When he returned to England he was stationed at the Haven Cliff, Seaton, CG station until his retirement in 1945. He was a member of the Seaton branch of the British Legion, and became the branch Standard Bearer. A quiet and courteous man, Lyons died in 1952 after giving a life of service to his country.

*Right:* Seaton girls in fancy dress costume, c. 1919. They are, from left to right: Joan Aplin, Joyce Baker, Violet Good.

Dr Tonge, his son Ken and friends from Beer on board the battleship HMS Rodney, which visited Seaton and Beer in 1928.

The Beer Lavender Fête, 1925. Dressed in costume were, from left to right: Dr Tonge, the famous Beer artist John White, whose paintings are now sought after by collectors, Dr Tonge's son Kenneth, and his daughter Leila.

Donald McKay-Ohm, MA, a graduate from St John's College, Cambridge, took over as headmaster at Colyton Grammar School in 1919 during the closing stages of its three-century-long life in the old School House in Colyton. It was a particularly troubled time for the school. Four of its previous seven heads had been asked to leave, the school had been closed twice in the previous forty years and, as well as still suffering the ravages of the First World War, serious overcrowding and primitive sanitation facilities had reached crisis level. Mr McKay-Ohm, irreverently but affectionately known as 'the Old Man' to his pupils, fought tooth and nail for the school, and gave authority no rest in a seven-year battle for a new and bigger school, until it was provided at Gully Shoot, Colyford. He also played a major role in the new school's development. He retired in 1949 after thirty years' service, the longest headmastership since the eighteenth century, and today's widely acclaimed school is a lasting testimonial to him and the sound foundations he built for it.

St Gregory's, Seaton, parish church choir, c. 1948. The vicar, Revd H.R. Cooke, is pictured here standing in the middle of his choir.

*Above:* The Pam Pam restaurant, on the Seaton Esplanade, where customers sat on Lloyd Loom chairs, now fashionable again. This photograph of staff members was taken in 1955. In the front you can see Harold Richards, with the peaked cap. Harold came from Axmouth, and in his younger days was a keen cyclist. In 1938 he cycled from Axmouth to East Grinstead in one day.

*Above:* Before the First World War, Cosens and Co.'s steamers from Weymouth made frequent calls at Seaton during the summer season. One of the passengers pictured leaving Seaton in 1905 was Mr J.N. Webster, on the right, smoking a pipe. Mr Webster, who came from Axminster, was later to become President of Axminster Hospital, and a Justice of the Peace. The lady in the front, with the splendid hat, was Mrs H. Cawley.

*Right:* Fore Street, Seaton, c. 1930. Bertie, pictured here walking up Fore Street, was what is often described as a character. He worked at the Pole Arms for many years as 'boots', the servant who cleaned boots and carried luggage.

*Opposite below:* Staff of Seaton restaurant, Le Matelot, pose on the steps for this picture. Among the group are Nina Snell, Geoffrey Wilder and Harold Richards.

*Above:* Axmouth School, 1921. Back row, from left to right: Alec Summers, Ken Critchard, Ken Webber, Tom Morgan, Cecil Ostler, Joe Poole, Mick Dack, Oliver Perry, Hedley Clement, Jack Critchard, -?-. Middle row: Mr Borne (headmaster), Dorothy Webber, Doris Critchard, Amy Clement, -?-, Lucy Waller, Olive Perry. Front row: Eric Bourne, Bertie Bourne, Kitty Start, Daisy Start, Beatie Vincent, Nancy Dean, Margaret Puddicombe, Queenie Morgan, Ada Richards, Florrie Richards, -?-.

*Left:* George Clarke of Beer, pictured here, died in 1947 at the grand age of ninety-six. He was a remarkable man, loved and respected by all who knew him, and because of his trade went by the nickname of 'Painter Clarke'. On his ninetieth birthday he walked from Beer to Bovey House carrying a ladder and a pane of glass to repair a window. He was still doing the odd job until he died, and during his ninety-fourth year papered the rooms in his grand-daughter's house. During his younger days, if short of work he would walk down the village of Beer with a ladder over his shoulder, and by the time he reached the beach would have enough jobs to last months.

*Above:* Threshing machine, Bolshayne Farm, Colyton Hill, 1898. Those included in the photograph are, bottom row: James Froom (nephew), MaryAnn (Polly) Sweetland (daughter), Samuel Sweetland (son), Robert Sweetland, 1830-1911, farmer of Bolshayne, with men from Colyton.

*Right:* Col. Gifford and his wife Muriel, c. 1939. Muriel Gifford, who died recently, was the daughter of Mr W.H. Head, a member of one of Seaton's oldest familes.

*Above:* Shooting the seine, Seaton, May 1928. Mackerel seining, pictured here, was a summertime industry. Seining could not be done satisfactorily with fewer than four men, and sometimes, if the catch was big enough, it would take many more. The seine net varied in length from 200 to 300 yd and comprised two arms. The part between, known as the bunt, was marked by a large cork buoy. When mackerel came close to shore to feed on whitebait, the seine was thrown out in a semi-circle and then hauled in to the shore.

*Above:* The Beer quarry team, c. 1885. This picture, painted by Stanhope A. Forbes, was exhibited at the Royal Academy.

*Right:* One of the bandsmen who played at the Beer Flower Show, August 1931. Any help in identifying the musician would be welcome.

*Opposite below:* Mr C.F. Gosney and his daughter Eileen, c. 1933. Mr Gosney, seen here walking along the Seaton Esplanade, was the town's chemist. His shop in Marine Place is now occupied by Byrne-Jones Photographic. Eileen Gosney, who died in 1988, devoted her life to researching the history of the Axe Valley, and was well known for her lectures on the area. She was a founder member of the Axe Valley Heritage Museum, which benefited from her years of careful research.

Beer quarrymen, c. 1896. Beer stone was used in Exeter Cathedral, Norwich Catholic Cathedral, Torbay Hospital and Lyme Regis church hall, among other places. It was considered to be the finest stone in the country for ecclesiastical work. The men who cut the stone from the caves by sawing it out in huge blocks worked in difficult conditions and were a tough and hardy breed.

Seaton Ladies Football Team, c. 1948. Back row, from left to right: Margaret Stentiford, Joyce Northcott, Margaret Billows, Rosemary Cochrane, Cecilly Holmes. Front row: Elizabeth Rodgers, Jean Hooper, Marion Searle, Beryl Denham.

*Five*

# High Days and Events

FREEING OF AXE BRIDGE

WAITING FOR THE DECLARATION

Ceremony to free Axmouth Toll Bridge, 30 September 1907. Although many photographs were taken of the ceremony, this one is of special interest. The grand old man standing in the front, with the buttonhole, was a Mr Hoare of Axmouth, who had this day celebrated seventy-three years of marriage.

Reading the proclamation of King Edward VII in Seaton Square, 26 January 1901. Queen Victoria died on 22 January 1901, and the successor to the throne was her son, the Prince of Wales. Here the people of Seaton listen to the chairman of the council read the letter from the Privy Council and the proclamation. The town band played the National Anthem and, for the first time in over sixty years, the crowd could sing God Save the King.

Performers taking part in a religious play in Seaton Town Hall, c. 1920.

*Above and below:* Queen Victoria's Diamond Jubilee celebrations, Beer, 1897. The possibilities of a great celebration in 1897 were first discussed after the Jubilee of 1887, although it was not until 1896 that public interest in the event was thoroughly aroused. Every town and village formed a committee to arrange activities for the great day, and everywhere the streets were lavishly decorated. Pictured here are the triumphal arches that spanned Fore Street in Beer, and some of the many fir trees that were dotted throughout the village. Processions, parties, sports and many other attractions were the order of the day, and the memory of this celebration stayed with people for the remainder of their lives.

*Above and below:* Colyton Fair Day, c. 1900. A fair and market as an exclusive right could be established only by Royal Charter, which specified its dates and duration. The Colyton market was granted in c. 1342 to Peter de Brewose, but the fair originated in 1208 when King John granted a fair at 'Culinton' to Thomas Bassett, to be held for seven days beginning in the octave of St Michael. The fair at Colyton was a gathering for buying and selling livestock which, before railways and improved road services, was a necessity of life to local farmers. It also gave them time for a chat about how bad things were.

*Above:* Members of Colyton's Mothers Union gathered to pose for this 1925 photograph.

*Below:* Empire Day celebrations, Colyton, c. 1908. Before the First World War, the townspeople always assembled to celebrate Empire Day, and flags were hung from first-floor windows along the streets. Pictured here we see the band leading the parade through Queens Square. Life was more leisurely in those days, and days like this were highlights in the year's calendar.

Pictured here on 1 February 1922 are members of the Seaton and Colyton Operatic Society, who performed Gilbert and Sullivan's Mikado that year.

Colyton Coronation Committee, 1911. Pictured here are the worthies of Colyton who organized the events in the town for the Coronation day of King George V and Queen Mary.

Colyton, c. 1934. A frustrating feature of the work of a museum curator responsible for collections of old photographs is that some turn up with no date or subject matter. This picture falls into that category and, although the people are recognizable, the exact date and occasion remain unknown.

HMS *Pinafore*, Colyton, 1921. At the time of this picture, Gilbert and Sullivan operettas were already classics, and nearly every town in the country had its local society devoted to an annual production. Today Gilbert's comedy is faded and old-fashioned, yet Sullivan's tunes enjoy perennial youth.

Christening the *Ruby*, a Beer drifter, Beer beach, 1925.

Coronation celebrations, Ferris and Prescott, Seaton, 12 May 1937. Ferris and Prescott, the drapers, traded successfully in Queen Street for over forty years until the retirement of Mr Ferris in 1974. Mr Ferris is pictured here, standing in front of the shop with his staff, on the Coronation day of George VI. The premises had been decorated for the occasion.

Early arrivals waiting to see Axmouth Bridge declared free, 30 September 1907.

Beer, 1926. Fisherman William Rowe demonstrating the use of the cork life-jacket at a life-saving apparatus drill in the presence of the local inspector of coastguards.

The 1953 Seaton Carnival was organized by the Seaton Football Supporters' Club and the local British Legion branch. Pictured in Seaton Town Hall is the Carnival Queen for that year, Miss Sheila Tolman. Her attendants were Miss Josie Hawker and Miss Sheila Hutchings. Standing on the left is Mr Norman Tolman, who was carnival chairman that year, and the queen's father. The lady on the right is local doctor's wife Mrs Coburn, who performed the crowning ceremony. Tragically, Sheila Tolman was to die from cancer within a few months.

*Opposite above:* The 1949 Seaton Carnival was a great success. Included in the tableau pictured here, which was entered by the Pole Arms, are the locals Arch Gigg, Gordon Clements and Joan Simpson.

*Oppsite below:* Presentation of a cup to a Seaton Carnival class winner by the Carnival Queen, Miss Murial Hawker, c. 1948. At that time, Seaton Scouts organized the local carnival, and standing at the rear of this photograph you can see Scout-master Skipper Brooks. The two attendants were Miss Sheila Lee and Miss Margaret Billows.

Laying the foundation stone, Feoffees' Town Hall, Colyton, 5 January 1927. On 13 May 1924 it was decided that a public building for the benefit of the town should be erected by the Colyton Feoffees. Great interest was shown when the foundation stone was laid by their chairman, Mr E.H. Cuming. After the ceremony Mr A. Lucas, the architect, presented him with a silver trowel. Photographed here are: 1 Mr Hooper (a mason), 2 Mr Lucas (the architect), 3 Mr Marsh, 4 Mr F. Wood, 5 Mr Long, 6 Mr E.J. Bastable, 7 Mr H.B. Strawbridge, 8 Mr G. Sprague, 9 Mr J. Follett, 10 Mr H.J. Loveridge, 11 Mr E.H. Cuming, 12 Revd H.S. Wyatt, 13 Mr J. Zeally, 14 Mr T.D. Harris (the bailiff), 15 Mr R. Richards.

Tree planting ceremony, Harbour Road, Seaton, 1954. In 1954, Harbour Road was known as Station Road, and in an attempt to make the area more attractive the Seaton Rotary Club financed the planting of trees. Pictured here, outside the old Geisha Café, are, from right to left: Ben Turner, Revd H.R. Cooke, Arthur Thorn planting the tree, Frank Norcombe, Len Chard -?-, Dr Maclean, John Morgan, -?-, Charlie Taylor, George Trevett, Dentist Burnside, -?-, A.N. Burgess, Miss Archer.

*Left:* Colyton's St Andrew's church is one of the best parish churches in Devon. Among its many treasures is the magnificent west window, seen here in October 1933 shortly after a disastrous fire gutted the nave and the aisles. Happily the restorers knew their job and the grand old church was fully restored to its former glory.

*Below:* This picture was taken after the fire which caused much damage to Colyton church in 1933. The fire was caused by an electrical fault.

*Right:* Firemen tackling the blaze at Colyton church, October 1933.

*Below:* The end of the Lion Inn, Colyton, 8 November 1908. Crowds had gathered to watch the old Colyton fire-engine make a futile attempt to put out the fire. The Lion Inn, which stood on the corner of Sidmouth Road, burnt down and was never rebuilt.

*Above:* Colyton Carnival children's fancy dress, 1971. The winners, pictured here, were 1st Matthew Moore, 2nd Catherine Skinner, 3rd Reuben Board, 4th Alexandra Carlyon. You can also see Colyton Carnival Queen, Darna Sparks, talking to Ken Harris. The others in the picture were Alwyn Brice, Percy Trivett, Mrs Board and Mrs Moore.

*Left:* Seaton Rotary Club President's Night at the Dolphin Hotel, Beer, c. 1971. Those present included Mr D. Isgrove, Mr C. Chubb, Mr R.F. Chapple and Mrs A. Clare.

*Opposite above:* Miss Ann Bellers of Colyton, crowned Queen of Seaton Regatta by Father Neptune in 1948. Behind her, holding the microphone, stands Bill Hatchley, one of the organizers.

*Below:* Pictured in 1972, this is the Chairman of Seaton Urban District Council, Mr George Clare, wearing his chain of office, boarding a Royal Navy ship which was on a courtesy visit to the bay. Others present include Mrs Clare, Mrs Sybil Clapp and Mr R.F. Chapple.

Beer WI folk dancing team, 1932. The team are pictured here with the trophies they had won that year: the Sidford WI Shield, the Beer WI Silver Cup and the Axminster Group WI Banner.

Beer WI pantomime, December 1932. The members of Beer WI performed *Cinderella* for the Christmas pantomime of 1932; pictured here are the ugly sisters.

Opening ceremony of St Clare's Adult Education Centre, 1 July 1971. St Clare's proved to be a worthy successor to the Stella Maris convent and became a focal point for community life with a programme catering for all age groups. Pictured here are the officials at the opening ceremony. Left to right: Mr Eric Jebson (exhibition organizer), Brig. G.L. Lillies (assistant secretary, Music Festival), Mrs C.H. Dixon, Mr C.H. Dixon (principal of the East Devon Technical College, Tiverton, who officially opened St Clare's), Mr F. Davis (chairman, Seaton Urban District Council), Mrs S. Clapp (chairman of the organizing committee), Mrs B. Buckley (committee member), Mr G. Lillies (secretary), Mr W. Buckley (exhibition chairman), Mr A.J. Vickery (St Clare's first warden).

Silver Jubilee celebration, the Esplanade, Seaton, 1935. At the close of the twenty-fifth year of his reign, the whole country united in what appeared to be one gigantic street party to thank George V for the sure guidance he had given to his people. Here you see the children of Seaton, dancing around the maypole on Seaton sea-front, in a part of the local celebrations.

George V Silver Jubilee, Seaton sea front, 1935. Taking part in the celebrations were the 1st Seaton Girl Guides, pictured here on parade.

George V Silver Jubilee celebrations, Colyton, 1935. Here we see some of the helpers who prepared the tea for Jubilee Day in the Colyton Feoffee Town Hall. They include: Kitty Hooper, Mr Sprague, Reg Gladman, Mr Bastable, Mrs Bastable, Mrs White, Miss Saunders, Miss Snell, Mr Copp, Mrs Copp.

The Coronation celebrations of George VI in Lower Church Street, Colyton, 1937. Lower Church Street was disrespectfully called Tiger's Bay by most Colytonians.

Inspection of Beer coastguards, c. 1898. The inspection was carried out by the area officer and the upright bearing of the men must have ensured full marks. A few years after this photograph was taken the cottages on the left were demolished.

Capt. W.H. Percy-Hardman taking the salute on Seaton sea front, November 1939, when the 4th Bn Devon Regiment, 'C' Coy, embarked for Mesopotamia.

*Grey Goose* MV on Beer Beach, c. 1929.

Beer Regatta, c, 1923. One of the features of pre-war Beer regattas was a prize for the best decorated boat, and pictured here is one of the prize-winners.

Seaton, 1914. At the outbreak of the First World War, the normally quiet seaside town of Seaton became a continuous scene of bustle and excitement. The steady enrolement of men proceeded week by week, and in this picture we see some of the first to join the Devonshire Regiment marching down Sea Hill during the late summer of 1914. We do not know how many of them came back, although we known only too well that the best of their generation died and those who did return found England had changed beyond recognition. Over 200 men from Seaton served in the war, and of these twenty-four made the supreme sacrifice. Their bodies lie in many lands, beneath many seas, but their names are recorded on the memorial cross which stands by the entrance to the parish church, reminding all future generations of what they gave, fighting for a cause they believed would bring a better world.

*Opposite above:* Laying the foundation stone of the Seaton Congregational church in Cross Street, 21 September 1894. This new church was completed during the following year, and was opened on 26 September 1895. The opening services of the Sunday school took place on Thursday 12 November 1896 with a divine service, followed by a public tea in the new school room. During the early years both church and Sunday school were well supported.

*Opposite below:* Pictured here in 1937 is the butcher's shop of T. White & Sons in St Andrew's Square, Colyton. The shop was decorated for the coronation of George VI.

Rocket practice at Beer Quarries, September 1932. There were about four practice calls a year, and these always attracted a number of spectators. In this picture we see the coastguard arriving with the wagon which held all of the gear. During practice, a large rocket would be fired towards a mast. A light rope was attached to the rocket, and if it successfully hit the mast, a thick hawser was then attached to the rope and hauled aboard.

Formal opening of Beer Miniature Rifle Club, c. 1912. In this picture we can see the officials firing.

Empire Day celebrations, Colyton, 1909. Before the First World War, this was a school holiday, and an occasion of much rejoicing. Empire Day was held on Queen Victoria's birthday on 24 May. It originated in commemoration of the assistance given by the colonies in the Boer War of 1899–1902. Here we see the people of Colyton outside the post office, which was then run by Mr F.C. Brown.

Peace and Victory Committee, Colyton, 1919. In February 1919 a public meeting was called in the town to elect a committee to organize the local Peace and Victory celebrations. The First World War had ended on 11 November 1918 at 11 a.m., and it was decided to hold peace celebrations throughout the country on 19 July 1919. Pictured here are members of that committee in Colyton, including Mr Bowden-Smith, Mr Brokenshire, Mr G. Sprague, Mr Reg Wood, Revd Mr Molyneux, Mr S. Long, Mr E. Sellars, Mr Collins, Mr H. Hooper, Mrs White, Mr E.H. Cummings, and Mrs Long, with Mr Scott Evans and Mr T. Harris in the front.

Beer Boy Scouts, c. 1919. Scouting, with its organized games and bathing, instilled self control, fair play and manliness into boys throughout the world. The movement was received with great enthusiasm in Beer, and at the time of this photograph the troop numbered about fifty.

Jubilee celebrations, Colyton, 12 May 1935. The celebrations were sincere and heartfelt, and every street in Colyton was decked out with red, white and blue bunting. The schoolchildren were given special mugs and, as you can see in this photograph taken outside the Feoffees' Town Hall, Union Jacks were the order of the day.

Celebrations in St Andrew's Hall, Colyton. Possibly a Silver Jubilee or Coronation party in the 1930s. Any help with identification would be appreciated.

Standing on the right of this picture is Arthur Stenner, who was then Chairman of Seaton Urban District Council. He was presenting awards at the Seaton Autumn Show during the mid-1960s. Standing next to him is show secretary Jim Cross.

St Andrew's church bell-ringers, Colyton, 1907. Back row, from left to right: W. Rousell, G. Crabb, C. Barrett, S. Salway. Front row: J. Matthews, G. White, J. White, E. Facey, J. Newbery.

Gilbert Hutchings and Kings Arms landlord, Dick Spiller, are in the centre of this photograph, taken in Seaton's Kings Arms in about 1971. Any more information on the event would be welcome.

In 1951 the Seaton Town Hall was still out of commission, due to previous fire damage, so the carnival was centred in a marquee on the Seaton cricket field. The carnival was organized by the British Legion and the Football Supporters' Club. Pictured here in the marquee is the Carnival Queen, Miss Mary Gooding, with her attendants Marion Powling and Barbara Newton. She was crowned by Mrs Shand, the lady sitting on the left, who was accompanied by her husband Roy, on the right of the photograph.

Prince of Wales' visit to the West Country, c. 1925. Loved for his charm, his humility and his good will, the prince received an ecstatic reception wherever he went. Everyone wanted to get close to him and to touch him, so that by the end of these visits he was often covered with bruises. Pictured here is a large party of people from Colyton who went on an outing to Ham Hill, near Stoke-under-Ham, to welcome the prince.

Empire Day, Colyton, 1909.

Colyton Fête, 1909.

Coronation Day celebrations at Colyton, 1911. This photograph shows the people of Colyton getting ready to celebrate the coronation of King George V. The long trestle tables, seen here in Market Place, were in preparation for the high tea later in the day. The building on the right was the Shambles or Market House, which stood on the site of the present Feoffees' Hall.

REV. R. TURNER'S FAREWELL SERVICE TO THE COLYTON VOLUNTEERS

Revd R. Turner's farewell service to the Colyton Volunteers, c. 1914.

George VI Coronation celebrations, Colyton, 1937. The people in the photograph include: Reg White, Frank Wood, Roby Loveridge, Mrs Loveridge, Mr Bastable, Jack Snell, Mr Horner, Frank Davey, Fred Warren, Fred Hoare, Mr Jenkins (schoolmaster), Bert Long, Mr Brokenshire, George Thorner (Jobie), Sidney Richards, Henry Hooper, Ned Hoare, Ern Hussey, Ern White, Mr Copp (blacksmith), Bert Copp (baker), Alfie Weston, Jack Boles, Miss Shell, Alice Aldred, Mrs Sansome, Bert Hussey, Dick Fox.

Stepps Lane, Axmouth, September 1960. This photograph is looking towards what was then the Stepps Country Club Hotel, after the cloudburst that caused severe flooding and havoc in the village.

A week of rain preceded the torrential downpour on 1 October 1960, and Axmouth suffered the worst floods in living memory. The flood-waters rushed through the village like a torrent, ripping up sections of the road and tarmac. More than forty houses took the brunt of the water, with ground floors covered in inches of black mud. Here you can see the debris left behind after the floods.

*Above:* Axmouth Club walk, c. 1900. About this date, nearly all the men who lived in the village belonged to a friendly society, which had the admirable object of assisting its members in time of sickness, and providing a sum of money at death. The annual club day was an event much anticipated by the villagers. It commenced with the club walk, led by a band, which the members followed carrying banners and poles festooned with bunches of flowers, which they waved about with much merriment.

Queen Victoria's Diamond Jubilee celebrations, Beer, 1897. Every street was decorated, coloured portraits were hung in every cottage window, and the event was blessed with continuous blue skies. A full programme of events was organized, which included sports, dancing and a high tea. The local people promenaded the village in parties, and everyone wore their best hats. Here we see the local coastguard, with the local naval reserves, leading the jubilee parade through Beer.

*Opposite below:* The meet of the Axe Vale Harriers at Colcombe Castle, Colyton, c. 1930. The Axe Vale Harriers met two days a week to hunt foxes and hares, with a season from the middle of September through to the middle of April.

*Above:* Wreck of the *Malpas Belle*, February 1922. The Malpas Belle was a Polish-registered barque laden with iron ore, and was wrecked between Seaton and Beer during a storm in February 1922. Fortunately no lives were lost.

*Left:* Beer Regatta Day, August 1937.

# Six

# Sportsmen and Sporting Events

*Opposite:* Seaton Football Club dinner at the Royal Clarence, c. 1951. Players and members here include Roy Rodgers, Don Rodgers, Harry Moore, Derek Real, Slack White, John Cockram, Brian Baker, Stan Pritchard, Gerald Gosling, G. Trevett, S. Carlisle, P. Westlake, W. Hutchings, N. Clark, Mr Haymes, H. Northcott, T. Beavan, G. Sellers, Mr Bastone, E. Haymes, G. Trevett, W. Hutchings.

Seaton Athletic Football Club, 1945-6. This is the team that drew 2-2 with Axminster Town in the first post-war Axminster Hospital Cup Final. They lost the replay 3-2. Back row, from left to right: -?-, Geoff Sellars, -?-, -?-, Steve Price (sen.), Steve Price (jun.), Wallace Anning, Frank Bridle, Harry Leyman, 'Bunny' White, Mr Ladd. Front row: Tommy Beavan, Jim Taylor, Maurice Bevan, Neville Lake, Horace Critchard.

Seaton footballers, c. 1948. Back row, from left to right: -?-, -?-, Percy 'Fritz' Miller, Jim Taylor, Wallace Anning, Ivor Real. Front row: Steve Price (sen.), Ted Denham, Reg Clarke, Tommy Beavan, 'Bunny' White.

Seaton Football Club, winners of the Axminster Hospital Cup in 1934-5, when they beat Crewkerne Unitarians 2-0 in the final with two goals from John White. Back row, from left to right: Vic Muggeridge, Jim Taylor, -?-, Percy 'Fritz' Miller, Bill Snell, Wallace Anning. Front row: George Trevett, Wilf 'Nippy' Ball, Cyril Watts, -?-, Ivor Real. Vic Muggeridge, who later played for Colyton, went on to become the secretary of the Perry Street & District League for nearly forty years, and is now the league's president.

Seaton Town Football Club, 1954-5, winners of the Seaton Supporters' Cup (later Seaton Challenge Cup), beating Lyme Regis 2-0 at the Colyford Road ground. Back row, from left to right: Bill Pritchard, Wilf Hutchings, Donald Rodgers, Syd Nicholls, Mike Martin, Harry Moore, Alan Hayes, Ron Anning, Hermon Anning, Arthur Critchard, Tom Hamm, Syd Carlisle. Front row: Brian Baker, Derek Real, Len Pritchard, Ivor Anning, Jim Anning. Front: Keith Hamm (mascot).

Beer's comic football match, c. 1955. Back row, from left to right: John Driver, John White, Eric Kenworthy, Frank Russell, -?-, Basil Lang. Front row: Rosemary Abbott, Flip Restorick, -?-, Peggy Turner, Mary Burridge, Margaret Wilkins, Eunice Smith, Rita Somers, Pam Hitchcock, Doreen Bastone.

*Opposite below:* Colyton Football Club, 1922–3 season. Back row, from left to right: Mr Ellis, Mr Bastable, Donald Baker, Billy Hann, Bert Warren, Fred Hoare. Front Row: Charley Facey, Bill Salway, George Fry, Freddie Hoare, Kinger White.

*Above:* Colyton Football Team, winners of the Morrison Bell and Lyme Hospital cups, 1924–5. Back row, from left to right: George White, Reg White, Dan Woodgate, Bill Solway, Donald Baker, Mr Jarvis, Mr Swatridge, Bill Littley, Bill Hooper. Centre row: Charlie Facey, Bert Warren, Harry Strawbridge, Ollie Bastable, Mr Ellis. Front row: Bert Copp, Georgie Fry, Billy Han, Wilf White.

Axmouth School Football Team, 1932. Back row, from left to right: Ben Newberry, Peter Real, Maurice Webber, Douglas Morgan. Middle row: Horace Critchard, George Morgan, Arthur Ayres, Harry Morgan. Front row: Victor Morgan, Roy Webber, Phillip Soper.

Axmouth United AFC Ladies Football Team, Flower Show week, 1948, pictured at the old football ground in the village. Back row, from left to right: Emmie Johns, Betty Widger, Mary Webber, Win Maidment, Betty Furzey. Front row: Dinah Millman, Irene Beasley, Eleanor Newberry, Kathy Ostler, Margaret Northcott, June Sweetland.

Seaton Town Football Team, c. 1948.

Seaton Football Supporters' Club committee, taken at Warner's Camp, Seaton, c. 1951. They are, in the back row, from left to right: Mr W. Hutchings, Mr H. Northcott, Mr T. Beavan, Mr H. Northcott, Mr D. Taylor. Middle row: Steve Price, Jack Taylor, Sid Nicholas, Mrs E. Haymes, Mrs Fillbrook, Wilf Hutchings, Fritz Miller, Wallace Anning. Front row: Mrs E. Hutchings, Mrs Mary Jones, Admiral Sir Francis Pridham, Mrs B. Miller, Mrs F. Northcott.

Seaton Football Club committee, c. 1952, taken in the Pole Arms. Back row, from left to right: H. Anning, S. Nicholas, G. Sellers, F. Miller, P. Bowden, F. Sellers, D. Taylor. Front row: G. Trevett, Mr Pilchard, G. Hutchings.

*Opposite above*: This was presumably a Seaton sports club dinner, taken in the 1960s. Mr G. Trevett and Mr Paul are sitting at the top table with all the season's cups.

*Opposite below*: Seaton Darts League champions c. 1965. Back row, from left to right: Peter Dack, Dave Dack, Terry Fox, Sam Searle. Front row: Cliff Farmer, Ron Anning, 'Mac', Don Chubb.

Seaton Rugby Football Club, 1900–1 season. Players pictured here include Tom Rodgers, Dicky Skinner, Bill Real, Billy Head and Dr Monty May. The man on the right with the flag was Harry White, and the short man on his right, with the satchel, was called 'Cycle' Jones, whose family owned Jones Bazaar, now The Paper Shop.

*Opposite below:* Axe Cliff Golf Club House, Seaton, c. 1919. The course consists of eighteen holes, and its position on the summit of Haven Cliff gives magnificent views from Portland Bill to Start Point. The president at that time was Sir Wilfred Peek, Bt, and the professional was Ernest Hoare of Axmouth. The club celebrates its centenary in 1994.

*Above*: Seaton, Axe Cliff Golf Club Cup winners, c. 1965.

Seaton cricket, c. 1903. Viewed across nearly a century of war and economic crisis, the England of Edward VII appears to have been a place of peace and prosperity, and this photograph captures the atmosphere of that brief Indian summer. This picture came from Gwendoline Marsh's album, and we see her sitting in front on the right. Gwendoline was a member of a solid, established professional family, her father was a solicitor in Yeovil, and they came to Seaton every year for a month's holiday. Seaton then, as now, had a first-class cricket ground where, during the summer, travelling and local teams competed with the visitors. Here the Marsh family and friends pose for a charming photograph, taken during the tea break.

*Opposite above:* Seaton Bowling Club, team winners with cup, c. 1960. They are, from left to right: Mr E. Gilbert, -?-, Mr Paul and Mr N. Tolman.

*Opposite below:* Beer Miniature Rifle Club, c. 1910. The club was well supported, and in this picture we see Mrs Marston at the formal opening, firing the first shot.

"Beer Miniature Rifle Club." Formal Opening. "Mrs Marstons Opening Shot.
Photo R.G.T. Wildbeer

Beer WI folk dancing competition, 21 July 1931. The team from the Beer WI dance 'Jack's Maggot' in the grounds of The Grange. The competition was won by them.

Seaton Cricket Club, c. 1908. The Cricket and Lawn Tennis Club attracted many visitors during the summer months. Pictured here outside the pavilion are players from the local team, with visitors.

Seven

# Transport

After the First World War, life in Devon became less isolated, with the coming of the motor-bus. Transport pioneers began local bus services in all areas, and were soon running charabanc outings to West Country beauty spots. Long before the national bus companies appeared, local firms such as Good's of Beer and Clapp's of Seaton were providing a good service. Pictured here in 1925 is a party of Seatonians leaving for Cheddar.

*Above:* Express Dairy Safe Driving Awards dinner, c. 1955. For over thirty-five years the name Express Dairy dominated the agricultural scene in East Devon, as milk and eggs were collected and taken by road to Seaton Junction. At its peak, the dairy employed over a hundred people, and their drivers were given awards for safe driving. These drivers were the company ambassadors, and rightly earned much respect from the farming community.

*Above:* Clapp's horse-drawn funeral hearse coming up Queen Street, Seaton, c. 1906. The house which stood at the junction of Beer Road was one of the oldest buildings in the town, and was demolished in the 1960s to improve the corner.

*Right:* Clapp's transport, Seaton, 1906. For most people eighty years ago this was the only way to go to your hotel. With luggage piled high on the top, the horse-bus passengers are eagerly looking forward to their stay at Seaton after the journey by steam train from London and the Midlands. It seems that they are en route for the Beach Hotel. The postcard picture is dated 1906, at which time old Tom Clapp had stables down at the Beach Hotel and ran horse-buses all over the place. He had the concession to run visitors from the railway station to the hotel along what was then Station Road, so the bus is likely to be one of his.

*Opposite below:* Old Beer Road, Seaton, c. 1895. You can see in this photograph how much erosion has taken place during the past hundred years. The man with the horse is taking a block of Beer stone to Seaton railway station for transport by rail.

Seaton station, April 1914. The first meeting of the Seaton and Beer Railway Company was held at the Pole Arms Hotel, Seaton, on 5 December 1863, and the line was opened on 16 March 1868. In this photograph we can see the original buildings. These were replaced in the 1930s with a station typical of the period, Southern Region concrete and brick style.

Great excitement at Seaton Junction, c. 1930. Apparently a train was left in the siding with the handbrake off, it ran away, smashed through the buffers and ended up down this bank.

Mr E. Bastable, the Colyton baker, is pictured here in 1933, standing proudly in front of his new Ford van. His younger daughter Betty is sitting at the wheel. Mr Bastable had the Berry Stores in Colyton, and was a high-class baker and confectioner, grocer and provision merchant.

Colyton coach trip, men only, c. 1922. One of the changes after the First World War was the coming of the motor-bus into all parts of Devon. Pictured here, at the start of a day's outing, are many well-known Colytonians. The drivers are unknown, but the passengers include: Colonel Henderson, H. Hooper, A. Hooper, F. Hooper, E. Hooper, P. Hooper, E. Smith, E. Bastable, W. Skinner, J. Snell, W. Snell, C. Snell, W. Critchard, J. Critchard, D. Solway, P. Solway, W. Clarke, W. Beer, W. French, R. French, F. Hoare, W. Hoare, C. West, J. Long, F. Long, A. Wright, P. Wright.

*Above*: Central Garage, Seaton, c. 1929. Central Garage stood on the site of the present post office. Standing next to the car in the garage is a well-known Seatonian, Mr Bob Hoskins, who died in about 1980.

*Above:* This delightful little girl standing by the Austin 7 in Fore Street, Seaton, is Beryl Smedley, the daughter of the man who started the Central Garage in Seaton.

*Right:* Seaton Reservists leaving by Clapp's transport to catch the special train at Seaton Junction, August 1914. They had answered the call 'Your King and Country needs you', and were now proceeding to barracks for a few days' serious training before leaving for France. Their journey to the battlefront was triumphal progress, and wherever they stopped the whole population appeared to be there, offering them bouquets, chocolates, bread, sweets, beer and

*Opposite below:* Maypole dancing was one of the colourful customs of rural England. In the summer of 1923 the white-frocked girls pictured here, with ribbons in their hair, were performers from Colyton. The formidable lady with the large hat would have been the person in charge. Judging by the driver's expression, he was not too happy with his lot, and was expecting trouble from these little angels.

Express Dairies, Seaton Junction, c. 1948. The milk churn and these lorries were once a daily sight outside every farm and along every lane and road in East Devon. The depot opened in 1933, and in 1948 the first road tanker was used to send milk to London. In the same year, the fleet of ten milk lorries pictured here were in use, and a new canteen for the work force was built.

Flooding in Harbour Road, Seaton, c. 1972. The car in front, going through the floods, belonged to the well-known Derek Oliver Good from Beer, and carried the distinctive number-plate DOG 2.

The Old Colyton fire engine, pictured here in 1937 with Derek Fox, Bill Long and Hector Turl in the front and Mr Solway and Mr Potter sitting in the rear.

Pack donkeys at Weston Gap, 25 August 1928.

Loading Beer stone at Seaton station, c. 1895. The stone from the quarries at Beer is of the calcareous type, and lies in so solid and thick a bed that blocks of any dimension can be cut from it without wastage. Stone has been excavated from these quarries for probably two thousand years, and has been used in many of the important old ecclesiastical buildings in the West Country. Peak House in Sidmouth was built entirely of Beer stone.

Motor accident on the Musbury Road, c. 1933. A group of interested cyclists gather to watch the police. The van belonged to Eastman's the butchers.

Doris and Peggy worked in the Express Dairy depot at Seaton Junction, and are pictured here in the 1950s on their smart new bicycles.

During the 1930s, Mr A. Heard contracted with local farmers to bring their milk into the Express Dairy depot at Seaton Junction. The lorry pictured here collected from Chardstock to Lyme Regis.

Charabanc trip to Seaton, c. 1923. This photograph, taken on Seaton's Esplanade, shows how the internal combustion engine had changed transport and social habits. By this date holiday-makers could visit the town on a day trip from all parts of the county.

Comic novelty postcards were very popular with holiday-makers. This card of 1910 showing Seaton's Flyer was by 'Cynicus', whose real name was Anderson Martin. The unconventional humour and satire is typical of his work.

*Eight*

# Bovey House

Bovey House, Beer, c. 1895. This fine old mansion was for many years the ancestral home of the Walronds. In one of the bedrooms there is a beautiful example of seventeenth-century plaster work; the ceiling is decorated with a design representing Charles II hiding in an oak tree, surrounded by Cromwell's soldiers.

*Above and left:* Bovey House. In 1908 Mr A.L. Radford obtained a long lease on the house and carried out a number of alterations. The sixteenth-century panelling in the dining room was inserted at this date. The fine overmantle came from Sherborne Castle. It bears the arms of Sir Walter Raleigh, who began the new building in 1592. The rest of the panelling is of an earlier date and comes from the east of England. The plaster ceiling in the hall was also added at this date; it is copied from an example formerly in North Devon. Also added in 1908 were the statues of a king and a bishop, now in front of the summerhouse in the forecourt. These also came from the east of England.

The earliest house at Bovey must have been either of wood, or half-timbered. Stone houses in the twelfth and thirteenth centuries were confined to the wealthiest and most important families, but by the fifteenth century they were more widespread. The quarries at Beer provided excellent building stone, which was much used in the Middle Ages. The oldest part of Bovey House is the west wing, containing the present hall. This large room replaces the medieval hall, which originally reached up to the roof. Some sixty years ago, part of the original roof was seen above the bedroom ceilings. It is stated to have been of the fifteenth century and could well have been part of a house completed in, or shortly before, 1438. A fifteenth-century house of this type would have been a long rectangular block with the hall reaching up to the roof in the centre. On the east side of the hall the screens passage, now represented by the lobby inside the porch, would run from the front door to the back. From this passage doors led on the one side to the hall and on the other to the service rooms – the buttery and pantry – and the kitchen. At the far end of the hall were the private chamber and bedchamber, one above the other, in the space now occupied by a later eighteenth-century staircase. The service end of Bovey House has entirely disappeared, but the main walls of the rest of the block still stand, apparently with much of the fine timber roof hidden above the later ceilings. The only other feature of this date is the doorway, now reset to form the outer door of the porch. This dates from the fifteenth-century and appears originally to have been an open archway. A porch projecting in front of the screens passage is a normal feature in houses of this type. The doorway was probably the outer arch, facing south, not west as at present. A porch of this type would often have a small upper room, used as a chapel. When the property passed to Lord Rolle, Bovey House ceased to be the main residence of the family. It passed from the Rolles to Lord Clinton, whose family still owns the estate. During the late eighteenth and nineteenth centuries the house was generally let, part of the north wing being separated to form the farmhouse. At times it stood empty. It was at this time that a local legend arose to the effect that the house and the lane leading up from Beer were haunted. Beer was one of the last centres of smuggling, and it is possible that the empty house was used on occasion for hiding contraband. Whether or not this was so, a reputation of this sort would be useful in keeping strangers away from the vicinity, and particularly from the lane, which must have been one of the more convenient ways of running the cargo into the house.

# Acknowledgements

I am grateful to all those who contributed valuable information in the compilation of this book. My thanks must go to Arthur Chapple, Harold Richards, Dick Illes, Michael Clements, Mrs Violet Webster, Gerald Gosling, John Godfrey, Norman Whinfrey, Mrs Ernestine Jowett, Roy Chapple and John Cochrane for allowing me to use material and helping me to obtain knowledge of times past.

Thanks must also go to Lyn Marshall, without whose help I could not have produced the book. Edna Everitt gave much appreciated assistance, and I am grateful to my wife for her encouragement and help, also to Simon Fletcher and Lucy Stringer of Alan Sutton Publishing Limited for their assistance.

Finally, I would like to say that the dates presented are correct in my opinion, and when accompanied by a 'circa' may be ten years out. Old photographs can truly be everybody's best friend; to live in them is never to die.

The choir of Seaton parish church, St Gregory's, pose in 1912 for this picture with the Revd R.S. Robinson.